Second Edition

A Quick Reference to

THE RESEARCH PAPER

Sharon Sorenson

AMSCO SCHOOL PUBLICATIONS, INC.,

a division of Perfection Learning®

Cover Design: Meghan J. Shupe
Design and Composition: Sierra Graphics, Inc.

Please visit our Web sites at: *www.amscopub.com* and
www.perfectionlearning.com

When ordering this book, please specify:
either **13525** *or* A QUICK REFERENCE TO THE RESEARCH PAPER
SECOND EDITION

ISBN 978-1-56765-183-6

5 6 7 8 9 10   15 14

Contents

Contents

Introduction

Here is a simple, easy-to-follow twelve-step guide for writing a research paper. The assignment to do a "research paper" may come under several labels.

Report

A report is usually a summary of only one or two sources that develops a topic but not a thesis. It provides information but does not argue a position.

Factual research paper

A factual research paper is an expanded report using multiple sources but still developing only a topic, not a thesis. The I-search paper would fall into this category.

Evaluative research paper

Most often teachers want an evaluative research paper, one that is developed from multiple sources but addresses problem-solutions, causes or effects, comparisons or contrasts, assessment, analysis, or interpretation. It supports a topic and a thesis and may reach a conclusion that expresses an opinion.

Term paper

A term paper is a paper written for a specific course during a specific semester—or term. The term paper can be anything from a simple report to an evaluative research paper. Be sure to clarify what is expected of you when an instructor assigns a term paper.

For any research assignment, it is essential that you understand the purpose and audience for your final product.

Step 1: Begin with a Schedule

Once you understand your assignment, before you lift a pen or head for the library, plan how you will complete the paper on time. Use the Time Management Chart on the following page to plot your work on a calendar. Then stick to your plan to make sure you finish on schedule.

Step 2: Choose a Topic

Your broad subject may be assigned. Even if it is, chances are you will need to narrow it to a manageable topic for the space and time you have to work. On the other hand, you may have to choose your own topic. For topic ideas, consult the daily media—radio, television, newspapers, the Internet. Consider your school-work and personal interests. Listen carefully to general conversations for they, too, may suggest topics. Choose a topic that holds high interest for you as it will help sustain your motivation throughout the writing process.

Time Management Chart

Weeks until final draft is due	10	8	6	4
Number of days to complete:				
Choose a Topic (Step 2)	4	3	2	1
Preliminary Work (Step 3)	4	3	2	1
Secondary Resources (Step 4)	5	4	3	2
Bibliography Notes (Step 5)	1	1	1	1
Primary Sources (Step 6)	5	4	3	2
Note Taking (Step 7)	10	8	6	4
Final Outline (Step 8)	1	1	1	1
Drafting (Step 9)	9	7	5	3
Revising (Step 10)	4	3	3	2
Final Draft (Step 11)	6	5	4	3
Proofreading (Step 12)	1	1	1	1

A good topic has these characteristics:

Interesting A good topic holds your interest and that of your audience; it's something you want to learn more about.

Manageable You have only a limited amount of time and resources available, so choose a topic you can handle.

Worthwhile Choose something of substance, something that matters to you. For example, writing about how fashion trends have changed over the years is far more meaningful than writing about a "cute" print on a shirt.

Original A good topic is not just a rehashing, for instance, of Abraham Lincoln's childhood. A more original topic might be how the books he read as a boy seem to have influenced his later political decisions.

Narrow the focus of your topic like this:

Avoid a topic that is **too broad**. The Ice Age is far too broad a topic, but the role of the Ice Age in the formation of the Great Lakes will work. Hieroglyphics is too broad a topic, but how original Egyptian hieroglyphics are protected will work.

By contrast, also avoid a topic that is **too narrow**, one for which little information is available. For example, discussing why a single YouTube video is popular is too narrow. However, discussing the characteristics that popular YouTube videos have in common to arrive at a conclusion of what appeals to a YouTube audience is a topic that has some breadth.

Avoid a topic that is:

Too ordinary Every driver's manual, for example, will name the same laws of the road, so the topic is too ordinary, or expected. Try to find a topic that is more complex and more thought provoking.

Too familiar You may get bored and you will miss out on the opportunity to explore and learn about something new.

Too technical Doing the research will keep you busy enough without your having to simultaneously learn a technical language. You may also forget about your audience's unfamiliarity with a topic, which can lead to writing where you assume your audience knows more than they actually do, which will only confuse them.

Too factual A research paper is not merely a recitation, for instance, of the facts of Thomas Jefferson's life. You should try to argue for a certain perspective so that your audience will stay interested.

Too new Since you need print and nonprint sources and since the Internet alone is inadequate for research, a too-new topic will have insufficient sources.

Choose a topic that you can word in a question, like these:

> How did Jefferson affect American politics prior to his presidency?
>
> How do the Amish differ from the Mennonites?
>
> How are the physical skills necessary for snow-boarding different from those necessary for surfing?

Wording your topic as a question ensures that you are, indeed, taking some sort of position on the subject. It also helps you to stay on topic as you write your paper because you can ask yourself the question after you write each paragraph, and if the paragraph answers at least part of the question, then you know you're still arguing your thesis.

Step 3: Do the Preliminary Work

Before you get down to serious business, do some preliminary work. In the long run, it will save you hours, maybe even days. The preliminaries consist of three parts:

1. **Do some preliminary reading** to get background information about your topic. This will give you an overview of the topic, help you to narrow your focus, and can often lead you to some helpful sources. Check one or more of the sources on the following page.

A GENERAL ENCYCLOPEDIA, like

> *The Encyclopedia Americana*
> *Encyclopedia Britannica Micropaedia*

A SPECIALIZED ENCYCLOPEDIA, like

> *Encyclopedia of Social Sciences*
> *Jewish Encyclopedia*
> *Encyclopedia of World Literature in the 20th Century*

OTHER GENERAL REFERENCES, like

> *News media*
> *Current Biography*

If you find, during your preliminary reading, that your specific topic is too complicated or yields an overwhelming amount of information, narrow your topic further by choosing just one area within your topic on which to focus your essay.

2. **Write a research question** that reflects the purpose of your paper, like these:

> How does filming a movie in 3D differ from shooting films in the traditional way?
>
> How has the music industry had to adapt because of the move from store-bought CDs to digital, downloadable content?
>
> Should the government be allowed to tax money and goods people receive as inheritance? Why or why not?

After you finish your research, you will answer the research question in the form of a thesis sentence. More on that later.

3. **Prepare a working outline.** The working outline guides your work, tells you in advance what specific information you need, and reminds you which materials you should spend time reading and which are irrelevant to your work. It works for you, directs your research, and helps you find your way toward an answer to your research question. Writing the working outline is a deductive thinking process. You have a general topic; it needs specific supporting details. What specific questions need answers to explain this big, general topic? Consider this example:

Research Question

> What effects does laser technology have on general surgical procedures?

Specific Questions

1. Does laser technology speed surgery?
2. How do doctors decide when to use it?
3. Is the technology readily available?
4. What special facilities are necessary?
5. Are most doctors trained to do laser surgery?
6. Does it speed recovery?
7. Is it better for some surgeries than for others?
8. Does it cost more than traditional surgery?
9. What dangers accompany laser surgery?
10. Do problems recur after laser surgery?
11. What damage can laser surgery cause?
12. Are there side effects from it?
13. What are the psychological problems before laser surgery?
14. Should the patient expect psychological effects afterward?
15. What effect does it have on the length of hospital stay?

Working Outline

From the list of questions, generate a working outline by grouping together similar ideas that will form the major sections of your paper. An outline based on the sample questions on page 7 will look something like this:

    I. Elements for success
       A. Medical facilities (questions 3, 4, and 5)
       B. Patient condition (questions 1, 2, and 7)

    II. Potential for problems (questions 9, 11, and 12)

   III. Cost to patient
       A. Direct
          1. Surgery (question 8)
          2. Hospital stay (question 15)
       B. Indirect
          1. Recovery time (questions 6 and 10)
          2. Psychological impact (questions 13 and 14)

Step 4: Locate Secondary Sources

With your working outline in hand, you are ready to look for sources of information. You may use two kinds of resources, listed as follows:

Primary Sources

    Materials that are contemporary to your subject—a book, an interview, a survey response, a letter, an e-mail. "Contemporary" means "at the same time as," so a primary resource for an essay on Shakespeare might include his other plays or Samuel Pepys's diary, which was written during the time that Shakespeare lived (see Step 6).

Secondary Sources

Materials that are not necessarily contemporary with their subject, like books, journals, and online articles about your research topic.

Depending on your purpose and your topic, secondary references may be sufficient.

Seek a wide variety of sources. A good researcher will use books, magazines, pamphlets, and newspapers as well as nonprint media such as audio, video, and electronic sources. For a paper of 1,500 to 2,000 words, plan to use a minimum of twenty to twenty-five resources, remembering that in the final analysis, not every resource will be as valuable as it seems when you first find it.

Evaluate the sources. Before you haul home, print out, or e-mail yourself dozens of sources, check them for validity. Are they up-to-date sources from reliable authors and publishers? Have you found sources by those considered to be experts in the field you are researching? Did you skim possible sources for their usefulness by checking headings or chapter titles, the table of contents, and/or the index to evaluate the potential for your purpose and audience?

Following is a list of common secondary resources you can use for your topic.

General References

Consider general and specific encyclopedias, indexes, almanacs, and dictionaries as you get started on research. From there, you can look at more specific sources like those that follow.

Computer Catalog

Use your library's computer catalog, either from home or in the library, to search for sources.

- Use keyword searches. Often, when you look at a source listing, the catalog will offer a list of similar sources. Check out this list as it most likely contains other useful sources.
- Look up headings broader than your topic.
- Do an author search for works by authors of sources you've already discovered.
- Read carefully and follow precisely computer catalog directions, usually found on an opening screen. Each system is slightly different, and each relies on different connecting words or symbols to make your search successful.

Periodical Indexes

A periodical index lists items from sources like magazines, newspapers, and journals. Use these tips to search periodical indexes:

- As with a catalog, use keyword searches.
- In order to find more information, look up headings broader than your narrowed topic.
- Follow through on "see also" and other cross-references.

NOTE

Often, even though you may be able to search a library catalog from home, you may not be able to access a source directly. For this reason, try to conduct searches, even for electronic material, at your library. That way, a librarian can also help you to navigate the catalog, which can be very detailed and sometimes confusing.

Think about using the library at a nearby college as these libraries are often designed specifically for research. Either way, you can print out your digital sources for a small fee or e-mail them to yourself to look at on your home computer.

Indexes

Specialized indexes usually suggest valuable sources. Some of the most common ones include:

Education Index
General Science Index
Biological and Agricultural Index
Applied Science and Technology Index
Social Science Index
Humanities Index
Art Index
Book Review Digest

Bibliographies

Check books or articles you have already discovered for lists of additional useful references. These often appear at the end of chapters and articles or at the back of books. Although these are available electronically, you will most likely not be able to access them from home, but you will be able to access them from a library.

Print or Electronic

Newspaper indexes Depending on the timeliness of your topic, you may find valuable information in current or archival newspaper indexes, including those on the Internet. At **www.newspaperindex.com** you'll find newspapers from around the world.

Non-book media Check any vertical files (files maintained by librarians that contain media on various general subjects) for pamphlets, government publications, and clippings. Check the audiovisual department for microforms, films, or other audiovisual references. If you searched the library catalog, these sources will be listed on your results page.

Other sources Always consider government agencies, associations, and museums, many of which have Web sites with valuable information or with links to other helpful sites.

Searching the Internet

When you go online to search for sources, if you are using a search engine like Google, check out the home page. Most home pages for search engines will include a section that will tell you how best to search for information on that engine.

It will also help you to try out different search engines. Not only will this help you to become familiar with different kinds of searches, but it will also be more productive as different search engines may give different results.

Once you get the results, remember that they are arranged by relevance. Some search engines might even give each source a relevance ranking. Click only on the first few links to see if the search is helpful. If it is, then read the short descriptions of the sites that the search engine provides. Click only on those that seem most relevant to your topic.

Be sure to narrow your search so that you don't get too many different sites. Follow these guidelines:

- Use multiple search terms.
- Add a limiting term. Instead of searching for "body language," try "reading body language."
- Choose a more accurate term. Use "nonverbal communication" instead of "body language."
- Start with the most important word.
- Use symbol or Boolean operators (see next section).
- Try searching within the sites that a search engine lists for you.

Using symbol or Boolean operators can make your search more effective.

Symbol operators tell a search engine how to use the words in your search.

- Quotation marks tell the engine to find all words that are enclosed.

For example, *"body language"* will search for these two words together and not for just *body* or *language*.

- A plus sign (+) tells the search engine to include the word that follows in the pages it finds.

For example, *gestures + meaning* will result in pages about the meanings of gestures instead of just the gestures themselves.

- A minus sign (–) tells the search engine to find pages where the word that follows does not appear.

For example, *communication – verbal* will yield results that are about communication but not about verbal communication.

- An asterisk (*) in a word tells the search engine to find results for the actual word and any other forms of the word.

For example, *hand** will yield results related to *handle, handling, handsome, handshake, hands, hand-held,* etc.

- The letter *t* or *title,* followed by a colon, tells the search engine only to give results where the title contains your search word.

For example, *t: eye contact* will only give you results that have *eye contact* in the title.

Boolean operators are words that help you to narrow your search. They are always written in all capital letters.

- AND tells the search engine to find words that appear together, like the plus sign in symbol operators.

Example: personal AND space

- OR widens the search, essentially allowing you to search for two separate terms at once.

Example: nonverbal communication OR body language

- ANDNOT tells the search engine to eliminate certain terms.

Example: communication ANDNOT spoken

- NEAR will have the search engine find words within ten spaces of each other.

Example: avoiding eye contact NEAR meaning

- Adding parentheses can allow you to use several operators at once.

Example: (body AND language) NEAR meaning

NOTE

While the Internet is a viable source, check out these concerns:

Validity Anyone can put anything on the Internet. Thus, you must be able to determine the validity of anything you take from that source, including

Authorship

Author background

Date of publication (or most recent update)

Purpose of Web site's sponsoring organization

Remember, if you cannot validate the information, do not use it for research.

Step 5: Prepare Bibliography Notes

When you have located adequate resources, prepare bibliography notes for each one. You can use a separate 3"x 5" note card for each source or you can create notes in a word processing program. If you follow these guidelines, your Works Cited page will be a snap (see model paper, beginning on page 63).

Author

- Begin the first line of the bibliography entry at the left margin.
- Indent all subsequent lines five spaces (hit TAB once).
- Begin with the author's name, written last name first, followed by a comma and the first name and, if given, the middle initial. If there is more than one author, give the first name in this format, but provide subsequent authors' names in regular order: first name followed by last name and not separated by a comma. Separate authors' full names with a comma.

Title

If the book or article is unsigned, begin with the title. Titles must be written as follows:

- Underline or italicize titles of books, periodicals, television series, radio programs, and movies.
- Place quotation marks around the titles of articles or titles of specific radio or television episodes.
- Capitalize words in titles correctly.
- Separate titles from subtitles with a colon.

Publishing Information

For **books**, include the following publishing information:

- List the place of publication.
- Follow the place of publication with a colon, a space, and the name of the publisher.
- Follow the name of the publisher with a comma and the year of publication.
- Follow the date of publication with the medium of publication (print, CD-ROM, Web, etc.).
- If the book was accessed on the Web, first give the overall name of the site, italicized and followed by a period, then write "Web," followed by a period, and then give the date you accessed the site.

For **magazines and newspapers**, include the following publishing information:

- Follow magazine or newspaper titles with the issue date. For newspapers, include the edition, separated from the date by a comma.
- List dates in the correct manner, listing first the day of the month, then the month, and then the year (write "n.d." if no date is available).
- Follow the date with a colon, a space, and the page number. For a newspaper, you need only give the first page, followed by a plus sign (+) if the article is longer than that one page (ex: B3+).
- Give the medium of publication (print or Web). If the information was accessed on the Internet, follow the title of the article with the title of the overall site. Then give the publisher's name, followed by a comma and the date of publication. Next, write "Web," followed by a period and the date you accessed the site, also followed by a period.

For **Internet sources,** include the following publishing information:

- Follow the title of the work with the title of the overall Web site, italicized.

- Follow the site title with the site's publisher or sponsor (write "n.p." if none is available).

- Follow the publisher with "Web" to indicate this was an online source.

- Finally, give the date of your visit, in the form of day, abbreviated month, and year, not separated by commas.

For **television programs or films,** include the following publishing information:

- For a television program, give the episode title in quotation marks, and then the program or series title, italicized. For a movie, start with the title, italicized.

- For a television program, follow the series title with the name of the network and then the call letters and city of the local station (if necessary), followed by a comma and the date of broadcast.

- For a movie, follow the title with the director's name. Then give the name of the distributor, followed by a comma and the year of release.

- End each citation with the medium accessed (television or film).

Punctuation

In addition to punctuation detailed previously, use periods correctly, as follows:

- Follow each item (author name, article or episode title, book or movie or program title, publishing information, publishing medium, and date) with a period.

- Use only one period when the author's middle initial is included.

- Omit the period after magazine and newspaper titles.

- Include a period at the end of any months you abbreviate.

- Use a period at the end of each bibliography entry.

Other Details

Include helpful information for yourself.

- If you used more than one library, list the name of the library where you found a source.

- For books, list the call number or e-mail a copy of the computer catalog search results to yourself.

- Write down the URLs of any online sources you used, or cut and paste them into your document.

- Make a brief notation about important features for key references.

Above all, be consistent with all matters of style, using the same abbreviations, same format, same punctuation style, and same capitalization style throughout all your bibliography notes.

The following model bibliography note cards should help you develop your own notes.

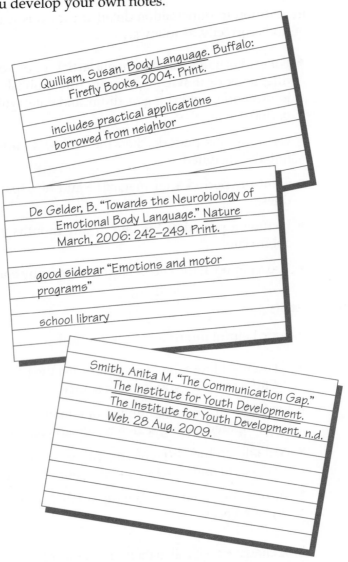

Quilliam, Susan. <u>Body Language</u>. Buffalo: Firefly Books, 2004. Print.

includes practical applications
borrowed from neighbor

De Gelder, B. "Towards the Neurobiology of Emotional Body Language." <u>Nature</u> March, 2006: 242–249. Print.

good sidebar "Emotions and motor programs"

school library

Smith, Anita M. "The Communication Gap." The Institute for Youth Development. The Institute for Youth Development, n.d. Web. 28 Aug. 2009.

The sample bibliography entries in the next section should help you use the correct form for a wide variety of situations.

Citing Sources

At the end of your research paper, you will include a Works Cited page, where you list the sources you used in the essay. Each citation must be formatted according to specific conventions. The conventions change depending on which kinds of citations you are creating, like MLA or APA. In this book, you are learning how to create citations in MLA format as these are the conventions used in most language arts classes. For a brief survey of APA format, see pages 79–80.

On the following pages, you will find the MLA citations format for different types of sources. Each type of source begins with a list of the information you should include; each piece of information is formatted correctly (ex: *italicized*) and is followed by the correct punctuation mark. After the list of information you need to include is an example of an actual citation.

BOOKS

Book by a single author

Author(s). *Title.* Place of publication: publisher, year of publication. Medium of publication.

> Hamby, Zachary. *Mythology for Teens: Classic Myths in Today's World.* Waco: Prufrock Press, 2009. Print.

Book by two authors
> Mortenson, Greg, and David Oliver Relin. *Three Cups of Tea: One Man's Mission to Promote Peace . . . One School at a Time.* New York: Penguin Books, 2006. Print.

Book by three authors
> Taylor, Robert W., Eric J. Fritsch, and Tory J. Caeti. *Juvenile Justice: Policies, Programs, and Practices.* New York: McGraw Hill, 2006. Print.

Book with four or more authors

If a book has more than three authors, give the first author's name and then write "et al." Follow all other conventions for citing books.

> Titon, Jeff Todd, et al. *Worlds of Music: An Introduction to the Music of the World's Peoples.* New York: Schirmer, 2004. Print.

Book with an editor or editors

Substitute the author(s) with the name(s) of the editor(s), followed by a comma and "ed(s)." Follow all other conventions for citing books.

Browning, John Edgar, and Caroline Joan Picart, eds. *Draculas, Vampires, and Other Undead Forms: Essays on Gender, Race, and Culture.* Plymouth: Scarecrow Press, 2009. Print.

Book by a corporate author

Give the name of the organization as the author's name and then follow all the other conventions for a book.

The Culinary Institute of America. *The Professional Chef.* Hoboken: John Wiley & Sons, 2006. Print.

Work in an anthology

Author(s) of the selection. "Title of selection." *Title of Anthology.* Editor(s) or author(s) of anthology with first names first. City of publication: publisher, year of publication. Page numbers of selection. Medium of publication.

Freud, Sigmund. "The Uncanny." *Literary Theory: An Anthology.* Eds. Julie Rivkin and Michael Ryan. Malden: Blackwell Publishing, 2004. 418–431. Print.

Multivolume work

Author(s) or editor(s). *Title of Work.* Volume (written "Vol.") and number. City of publication: publisher, year of publication. Medium of publication.

Cunningham, Lawrence, S., and John J. Reich. *Culture and Values, Volume I: A Survey of the Humanities with Readings.* Vol. 1. Florence: Wadsworth, 2009. Print.

Government publications

Name of government. Name of agency. *Title*. City of publication: publisher, year of publication. Medium of publication.

> United States. Dept. of Energy. *The Impact of Increased Use of Hydrogen on Petroleum Consumption and Carbon Dioxide Emissions*. Washington: EIA, 2008. Print.

Article in a reference book

"Title of entry." *Title of book*. Edition (if any). Date of publication. Medium of publication.

> "A cappella." *Webster's II New College Dictionary*. 3rd ed. 2008. Print.

Two notes about reference-book bibliography entries:

1. Many reference book articles, especially those in encyclopedias, are signed, the name appearing at the end of the article. Sometimes only initials appear. In that case, the initials will correspond to authors listed either in the front matter or in the index. When articles are signed, include the author's name at the beginning of the bibliography entry.
2. No page number is necessary for alphabetically arranged references like dictionaries and encyclopedias.

Additional Notes

If a book has both an author and an editor, put the author's name first, and put "Ed." and the editor's name after the title. Below is an example of a citation for such a source.

> Faulkner, William. *The Sound and the Fury*. Norton Critical Edition. Ed. David Minter. New York: W.W. Norton & Company, 1994. Print.

If a book has a translator, insert "Trans." after the title, followed by the translator's name. Here is an example:

> Darwish, Mahmoud. *A River Dies of Thirst.* Trans. Catherine Cabham. New York: Archipelago Books, 2009. Print.

If the book is a particular edition, like a fourth edition or an expanded edition, provide this information after the book's title, followed by a period. Do not italicize the edition of the book. Following is an example:

> Modern Language Association of America. *MLA Handbook for Writers of Research Papers.* 7th ed. New York: The Modern Language Association of America, 2009. Print.

If the publication medium of the book is the Web or a PDF document you accessed on the Web, then follow the conventions for printed books. However, instead of writing "Print," provide the name of the site where you accessed the book (italicized), followed by "Web." Then give the date you accessed the book in the format of day, month, and year without any commas between them. An example follows:

> Eliot, Charles. *Hinduism and Buddhism: An Historical Sketch.* Vol. 3. London: Routledge & Kegan Paul, 2000. *Project Gutenberg.* Web. 24 Aug. 2009.

Sources without stated publication information

Use the following abbreviations when publication information is not included in the source:

n.p.	no place of publication given OR no publisher given
n.d.	no date of publication given
n. pag.	no pagination given

Insert the abbreviation in the bibliography entry at the point at which full information would otherwise appear.

MAGAZINES AND NEWSPAPERS

Article in a daily newspaper

Author's name. "Title of article." *Newspaper title* (no period at the end) Date of publication, edition (if any): page range (write the range if the article is on consecutive pages; if not, write the first page, followed by a + sign). Medium of publication.

> Johnson, Richard. "Bad 'Week' for Morning Joe." *New York Post* 26 June 2009, late city final ed.: 20. Print.

Article from a periodical

Follow the instructions from a newspaper, but remove the edition information (if any). Place a colon between the date of publication and the page number(s).

> Grann, David. "Trial by Fire: Did Texas Execute an Innocent Man?" *The New Yorker* 7 Sept. 2009: 42+. Print.

NOTE

If you use the online version of a newspaper or magazine article, you will need to provide some additional information. Provide the following:

Author's name. "Title of article." *Title of overall Web site.* Publisher or sponsor of site, date of publication. Medium of publication (Web). Date accessed.

Dugger, Celia W. "South Africa Embraces Study Critical of Health Policy." *New York Times.* New York Times, 25 Aug. 2009. Web. 2 Sept. 2009.

Editorial

Author's name (if given). "Title of editorial." Write "Editorial" to indicate you are citing an editorial. *Publication title* (do not follow with a period) Date of publication, edition (if any): page number(s). Medium of publication.

If you are using an online version, follow the conventions for online periodicals on the previous page. Remember to still insert "Editorial" after the title.

> "Cellphones and Driving: No." Editorial. *Los Angeles Times.* The Tribune Company, 21 Aug. 2009. Web. 31 Aug. 2009.

Letter to the editor

Writer's name. Write "Letter" to indicate this is a letter. *Name of Publication* (do not follow with a period) Date of publication, edition (if any): page number(s). Medium of publication.

> Riviero, Ross. Letter. *Daily News* 2 Sept. 2009: 26. Print.

If you are using an online version, insert the name of the Web site, the sponsor, the medium (Web), and the date you accessed the site, as shown in the editorial citation above. Be sure to still insert "Letter" after the writer's name.

ONLINE MATERIAL

Article on a Web site

Author's name (if provided, may also be the name of an organization). "Title of Entry or Article." *Title of Web site.* Publisher or sponsor of site, date article was published or updated. Medium (Web). Date site was accessed.

Mangels, Reed. "Vegetarian Nutrition for Teenagers." *The Vegetarian Resource Group.* The Vegetarian Resource Group, 14 May 2003. Web. 1 Sept. 2009.

E-mail message

Name of sender. "Subject Line of Message." A description of the message, including the recipient's name. Date of the message. Medium (E-mail).

Davis, Cindy. "Dog Shelter Fundraiser." Message to Michael Morse. 21 July 2009. E-mail.

OTHER SOURCES

Material on CD-ROM or DVD-ROM

Author's name (if the article is signed). "Entry Title." *Title of Publication.* Edition (if any). City of publication: publisher, year of publication. Medium of publication.

"Greek Mythology." *Encyclopedia Britannica.* Deluxe 2009 ed. Chicago: Encyclopedia Britannica, Inc., 2009. CD-ROM.

An introduction, preface, foreword, or afterword

Writer's name. Section being cited (Introduction, Foreword, etc.). *Title of Book.* "By," followed by the author's name (include editor/translator if necessary). City of publication: publisher, year of publication. Page numbers of section used. Medium of publication.

Stevens, Sufjan. Introduction. *The Best American Nonrequired Reading.* Ed. Dave Eggers. New York: Houghton Mifflin Company, 2007. xi-xviii. Print.

Illustrated book or graphic narrative

Author's name. *Title.* "Illus." to indicate you're introducing the illustrator, followed by the illustrator's name. City of publication: publisher, year of publication. Medium of publication.

> Robinson, James. *The Starman Omnibus.* Vol. 1. Illus. Tony Harris. New York: DC Comics, 2008. Print.

Review

Name of reviewer. Insert "Rev. of" to indicate the source is a review, followed by *Title of the Work Reviewed* (normally italicized), followed by a comma and "by" and then the author's name. If the item reviewed is a movie, follow the title with a comma and "dir." and then give the director's name. *Title of Publication where Review Appears.* After the publication title, follow the conventions for the type of source where the review appears (book, magazine, journal, etc.).

> Anderson, John. Rev. of *District 9*, dir. Neill Blomkamp. *Washington Post.* The Washington Post Company, 14 Aug. 2009. Web. 19 Aug. 2009.

Map or chart

Title. Insert "Map" or "Chart" to indicate the type of source you are citing. City of publication: publisher, year of publication. Medium of publication.

> *Map of the West Coast of Africa from Sierra Leone, 1830.* Map. Philadelphia: Finley, 1830. Print.

Pamphlet

Cite a pamphlet in the same way you would cite a book. An example follows for you to use as a model.

> Department of Veterans Affairs. *The Post-9/11 Veterans Educational Assistance Act of 2008.* Washington: Department of Veterans Affairs, 2008. Print.

Film

Title. Name of director, preceded by "Dir." (You can also provide the name or names of performers, screenwriters, etc. preceded by "Perf." or "Screenplay by" as appropriate.) Name of distributor, year of release. Medium (Film).

> *Cold Souls.* Dir. Sophie Barthes. Samuel Goldwyn Films, 2009. Film.

Radio or television program

"Title of the Episode." *Title of the Program.* Name of network. Call letters and local station (if needed), date of broadcast. Medium (Television or Radio).

> "The Middle of Nowhere." *This American Life.* Public Radio International. WBEZ, Chicago, 5 Dec. 2003. Radio.

Interview

Name of person interviewed (last name first). Write "Interview" to show this source is an interview.
Next, determine what the source is (book, film, etc.), and provide the information as you would for that type of source. For sources with an author, editor, director, or the like, move the person's name to after the title and precede the name with the appropriate abbreviation ("By," "Ed.," "Dir.," etc.). For interviews in print, provide page numbers after the date of publication.

> Davis, Miles. Interview. *Notes and Tones: Musician-to-Musician Interviews.* By Arthur Taylor. Cambridge: Da Capo Press, 1993. 11–18. Print.

Speech, lecture, reading, or address

Speaker's name (last name first). Title of speech or reading, if known (enclose in "quotation marks" or *italicize* depending on content). Location, city of event. Date of event. Type of event (lecture, speech, reading, etc.).

> Daneshvari, Gitty. *School of Fear.* Barnes and Noble, Lincoln Triangle, New York. 10 Sept. 2009. Reading.

Work of visual art

Name of artist (last name first). *Title of Work.* Date of creation. Medium (watercolor on paper, bronze, etc.). Location viewed or name of collection where work is housed.

> Van Gogh, Vincent. *The Starry Night.* 1889. Oil on canvas. Museum of Modern Art, New York.

Step 6: Use Primary Resources

Read your secondary references thoroughly enough to know which primary sources will be of benefit and how they can enhance your research paper. Then, considering your narrowed topic, purpose, and audience, think about the most likely possibilities for primary sources: interviews, surveys, experiments, and/or letters.

Interviews

Make an honest effort to seek available community resources. They will enrich your research. After locating a potential source for an interview, follow logical steps for the interview process.

- Arrange for an appointment.
- Prepare a list of questions to address your purpose and specific topic.

- Send a list of questions for the interviewee to read through ahead of time.
- Confirm your appointment by phone or e-mail close to the interview time.
- Prioritize your questions in case you run out of time during the interview.
- Conduct the interview in a timely, gracious fashion.
- Listen critically to the interviewee's responses and ask logical follow-up questions.
- Thank your interviewee at the end of the interview as well as in a follow-up letter or e-mail.

Surveys

If your purpose and topic suggest the need for it, plan and conduct a survey. Use these steps:

- Include questions seeking information directly related to your purpose and topic.
- Word the questions objectively.
- If necessary, provide for a way to identify the source of responses.
- Conduct the survey in a timely, polite fashion.
- Calculate the results fairly.

Experiments

If your purpose and topic suggest the need for it, plan and conduct an experiment. Follow these steps:

- Develop a clear hypothesis or theory to test with the experiment.
- Make sure that your experiment will prove or disprove the hypothesis.

- Gather accurate data and analyze it objectively.
- Reach a logical conclusion based on the data.

Letters

If your purpose and topic suggest it, write effective letters or e-mails to potential sources. Follow these guidelines:

- Ask for specific information relevant to your research question.
- Allow ample response time.
- Be sure to thank those who respond.

Finally, no matter which primary resources you choose to use, manage your time well. You should probably begin preparing (contacting sources, writing questions, designing experiments) as soon as you start your research process. Remember that you need to leave enough time for respondents to get back to you, for you to actually conduct an interview or a survey, and for you to analyze results.

Step 7: Take Notes

The following directives apply to note taking from print and nonprint sources, from electronic media or multimedia.

General Guidelines

Before you begin taking notes, number or color code your bibliography notes. You will use the number or color to code your notes to indicate the source from which they come. You can also divide your notes into different sections, one for each source. However, it may be better to divide your notes into different subjects in your research topic, or categories, as doing it this way could make outlining easier. If you organize your research notes by idea, then using note cards or color coding will work best.

- Use a separate note card (3"x 5" or 6"x 10") for each idea, even if you write only a few words on a card.

- If you're working on a computer, use a separate page or document for each idea. You could also create a table with a separate section for each idea.

- Be sure to identify the source each time you make notes, either by writing the number you've assigned to the source or by using a color code in your notes.

- While you may develop your own form of short-hand, use only abbreviations that will make sense to you later.

- Be sure to include the page number for the information in the source from which you are taking notes.

- If you are using note cards, on the top line of each card add a slug—a title that identifies the topic of the note and corresponds to a heading or sub-heading in your preliminary outline. If you are using a Word document or creating a table, label each category with a heading that corresponds to your outline.

As you work, strive for accuracy and completeness. Consider the following reminders about note taking.

Plagiarism

Avoid plagiarism. Plagiarism is literary theft, using someone else's words or ideas as if they were your own. It's a serious offense, usually with severe penalties attached—like automatic failure for the paper or even the course. To learn how to avoid plagiarism, study the following passages.

Original Passage

In the area surrounding Salem, Massachusetts, in 1692 and 1693 a number of trials were held to prosecute people who had been accused of witchcraft. At that time, practicing witchcraft was punishable by death. Because the community of Puritans who lived in the area recognized no separation between church and state, the law of their religion was also the civil law, and that is why a seemingly religious infraction became punishable in civil court. A total of 19 people were hanged for the crime of witchcraft and one man, named Giles Corey, refused to respond to the charges and was pressed to death as a result.

Various theories exist about what may have caused this episode in American history. The trials have frequently been referred to as hysteria, and some explanations point to jealousies and desires for revenge among the settlers who lived in the Salem area. Two of the more interesting theories point to a type of encephalitis people can contract from birds and a substance in barley that can cause hallucinations.

Plagiarized (Not Acceptable)

Puritans living around Salem did not see a separation between church and state. Their religious law and their civil law were the same, so even religious transgressions could be punished in civil court.

Reworded, Partly Quoted, and Documented (Acceptable)

By the end of the trials, many lives had been lost and many more had been disrupted by false accusations. Some people were convicted and executed and some died in jail. 19 people died by hanging and one man, Giles Corey, was even pressed to death because he "refused to respond to the charges" (Borenstein 3).

(Note that in the preceding example, exact words appear in quotation marks and, along with the reworded portions, are acknowledged by documentation at the end of the paragraph.)

Reworded and Documented (Acceptable)

Many people have tried to explain how the Salem witch trials could have happened. Some historians believe that the events were a form of madness, while others have written that people involved were simply covetous and greedy. Still other, more intriguing explanations involve brain disease carried by birds and bread that contained hallucinogens (Borenstein 3).

(Note this completely reworded passage omits exact words. Since it is a paraphrase, however, credit must be given to the source.)

Avoid plagiarism by following three rules:

> DO NOT use exact words from a source without putting them inside quotation marks and giving credit to the source.

> DO NOT reword a passage without giving credit to the source.

> DO NOT summarize a passage without giving credit to the source.

Kinds of Notes

Not all notes are alike. In fact, you will want to take advantage of a variety of different kinds of notes as they best suit your purpose.

Direct quotation notes use the source's exact words, exact spelling, and exact punctuation. If a word is misspelled or incorrectly used, add the word [sic], meaning "thus," to clarify that the error is not yours.

Remember to avoid excessive quotations, using them for less than 20% of your notes.

Use direct quotations only under these conditions:

- when an authority's words carry weight.
- when the quotation is concise and powerful.
- when it would be impossible to restate as effectively in your own words.

Use quotation marks every time you use an author's exact words; otherwise, you will fall into the error of plagiarism.

As you look at the following examples of notes, observe how the writer includes a heading to state the general idea or category for each set of notes. Also, see how the writer identifies the source by providing the source number, circled, in the upper-right corner. The writer also includes the page number where he/she found the information in the source.

⑯ pg. 7

Eye Contact

"[Eye contact] is connected with basic survival patterns, in that youngsters who could secure and retain eye contact, and therefore attention, stood the best chance of being fed and of having their needs satisfied."

Partial quotation notes are mostly summaries in your own words, quoting only some key phrase. These notes follow a few simple rules:

- Use the ellipsis (a series of three periods separated by a space between each, like this . . .) to represent the omission of a word or words. If the omission occurs at the end of a sentence, a fourth period serves as the end mark. Place this extra period directly after the last letter in the sentence (like this. . . .).

- Use brackets [like this] to insert your own words inside a quotation or to change a word form (for example, from usual to usual[ly]). Never use parentheses for brackets.

- Always remember to use quotation marks around the quoted material.

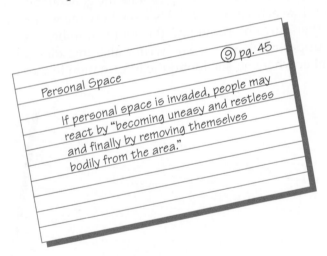

⑨ pg. 45

Personal Space

If personal space is invaded, people may react by "becoming uneasy and restless and finally by removing themselves bodily from the area."

Précis notes summarize in about one-third the length of the original. To be accurate, a précis must maintain the same tone and the same message as the original. Study the example on the next page.

Original Passage

Although teenagers usually have later bedtimes than their younger siblings, the teenagers actually need more sleep. While younger children need about eight hours of sleep, teenagers should be getting nine or more hours of sleep per night. Parents try to be understanding of their teens' seeming need to stay out late or to stay up late finishing homework, but these activities might be hurting their teens' health.

When teenagers stay up late during the week, they often need to catch up on sleep over the weekend. Teenagers' bodies, like bodies of any age, get set into a circadian rhythm, an internal clock that tells them when they want to go to sleep and when it is time to wake up. If teenagers sleep late on the weekend, the circadian rhythm is reset, so during the week, when they need to be awake early for school, their bodies get confused, thinking it is still time for sleeping.

Falling into this back-and-forth cycle, as many teenagers do, can be harmful in various ways. During sleep, important hormones for growth and development are released and so, if teenagers are not getting enough sleep, they may not be developing properly. Disruptions in sleep can also lead to poor performance in school and moodiness or depression.

Précis

Teenagers should be careful to keep their sleep patterns consistent so that they do not have to sleep in over the weekends. They should be getting about nine hours of sleep each night. If teenagers cannot maintain a sleep schedule, their school work can be affected, as well as their emotional well-being and their growth and development.

Outline notes may appear in formal outline style or look more like a list. In either case, these are particularly appropriate when noting a series of points or steps.

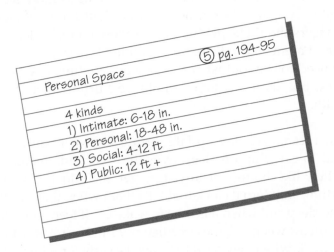

Personal Space

⑤ pg. 194-95

4 kinds
1) Intimate: 6-18 in.
2) Personal: 18-48 in.
3) Social: 4-12 ft
4) Public: 12 ft +

Paraphrased notes are a rewording of the original in about the same number of words; thus, they are most likely to lean toward plagiarism. Nevertheless, the paraphrased note is essential in two situations: when you need to simplify complicated text or when you need to clarify a passage. Study these passages:

Original Passage

For most of the twentieth century, the primary mediums for recorded music were vinyl records, tapes, or CDs. However, toward the end of the twentieth century and into the twenty-first, musical recordings became most popular in digital form, and they were downloaded onto MP3 players like iPods. This presented a problem for the music industry, which had made most of its profit from selling CDs and tapes for many decades. Today, the industry is taking a different approach to earning money. Record labels now collaborate with artists and launch extended tours to increase their revenue from ticket sales.

Paraphrase

During most of the last century, people usually bought their music on recorded media like vinyl, tapes, or CDs. At the end of the century and during this century, music has moved onto computers, and people can download songs and albums onto portable music players. That means that the recording companies lost much of their profit because people weren't buying CDs anymore. The labels have found a new strategy for turning a profit. They team up with musicians and send them on long tours to make money from the tickets people buy.

Combination notes combine any of the other types. They are probably the most useful and the most used.

(1) Combines
     outline
     and text

Communicating Openness   ⑨ pg. 160

If a girl wants a boy to ask her to dance she
  a) shouldn't try to look "cold and aloof"
  b) should smile and make eye contact
  c) should "make the boy feel comfortable and assured"

(2) Combines list with writer's
response

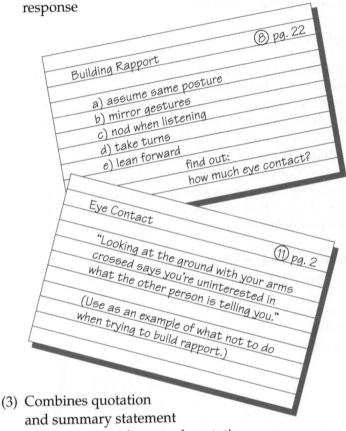

(8) pg. 22

Building Rapport

a) assume same posture
b) mirror gestures
c) nod when listening
d) take turns
e) lean forward

find out:
how much eye contact?

Eye Contact

(11) pg. 2

"Looking at the ground with your arms
crossed says you're uninterested in
what the other person is telling you."

(Use as an example of what not to do
when trying to build rapport.)

(3) Combines quotation
and summary statement
explaining significance of quotation

General Warnings

Finally, be alert to the following general warnings about note
taking.

- Avoid taking too many notes from only one or two
  sources.
- Use relevant, timely sources suitable for your
  topic.

- Take only notes that correspond to your working outline or to your revised working outline.
- Revise your working outline as your reading and note taking suggest.

Step 8: Write the Final Outline

You have revised your working outline as you have taken notes and found additional information or the lack of it. Now you need to make a final revision. Use the guidelines that follow.

Write a thesis sentence. Your thesis sentence answers your research question (see pages 5–7). Your outline must reflect your thesis. In other words, the sum of the parts of your outline must equal the thesis statement.

A thesis

- answers your research question.
- is a single declarative sentence with one main clause.
- states your position or findings on the topic.
- states the specific focus the paper will have.
- suggests what the conclusion will say.
- reflects what your notes provide.

A thesis is NOT

- a question.
- a statement beginning "The purpose of this paper is. . . ."
- a statement of the topic.
- made of multiple main clauses.

Examples:

Because people automatically make use of nonverbal messages in all face-to-face encounters, learning to send and interpret these messages accurately will improve overall communication at home, in school, with new acquaintances, and beyond.

While Steinbeck's depiction of the Great Depression in *The Grapes of Wrath* bears historical accuracy, at least one family showed little similarity between its life and that of the Joads.

Government, private organizations, and individuals are all working to solve what seems to be the insurmountable problem of homelessness.

Robotics of low, medium, and high technology have revolutionized industry by making it less dependent on but also safer for humans.

Sort your notes using the following plan:

- Sort the notes according to their headings—those topics that came from your working outline and that you used when you took the notes from your research.

- Check your notes for headings not on your outline and then decide if you need to add a heading or subheading or if you simply have irrelevant information.

- Check outline topics for which you have no notes and then decide if you need to change your outline or return to the library for more information.

Choose an organization pattern that will best reflect your purpose and topic:

1. chronological order
2. spatial order
3. order of importance

- from most important to least important (best for newspaper articles that the reader may not finish)
- from second most important to least important to most important (best for persuasive papers assuming a skeptical reader)
- from least important to most important (commonly used for general work, including research papers)

Check the structure of your outline. It should follow these guidelines:

Your outline must illustrate that you have divided the topic into relatively equal parts.

- To have six subheadings under one section and none under another suggests illogical division.
- To have eight examples under one subheading and two under another suggests that you might need to strengthen the latter.

The subheadings in your outline should relate to each other logically.

- Use headings and subheadings that are mutually exclusive. For instance, to categorize college students as male, female, and older is illogical.
- To categorize them instead as traditional and non-traditional, with male and female as subheadings under each, is logical.

Use logical divisions, divided by a single criterion.

- For instance, to divide pies into homemade, fruit, best restaurant, and recipes is illogical.
- Division by a single criterion, where pies are made, for example, is logical: homemade, restaurant purchased, or bakery purchased.

Avoid fifth- and sixth-level divisions for which you have nothing more than a sentence to write.

Maintain parallel structure. All topics within a level must be parallel to each other.

Study a model. The following is the outline for the model paper beginning on page 64.

THESIS STATEMENT: Because people automatically make use of nonverbal messages in all face-to-face encounters, learning to send and interpret these messages accurately will improve overall communication at home, in school, with new acquaintances, and beyond.

I. Nonverbal communication is automatic
   A. People do it as babies
   B. Parents communicate nonverbally
   C. May be automatic, but people need to learn to do it well

II. Submissive and dominant
   A. Submissive shows openness
      1. Smiles
      2. Nodding and bowing
   B. Dominance is aggressive
   C. When to use each kind of signal

III. Personal space
    A. Four zones
        1. Intimate
        2. Personal
        3. Social
        4. Public
    B. Signs space has been invaded

IV. Eye contact
    A. Used in infancy
    B. Shows openness or understanding
    C. Social eye contact
        1. Entering a room
        2. Recognition

V. Feet and legs
    A. Unconscious, so informative
    B. Leg positions
    C. Mirroring

VI. Arms and hands
    A. Closed and open
    B. Hand-to-face gestures
    C. Reading in job interviews

Analyze the Model Outline

The six main headings, when added together, equal the thesis statement.

$$I+II+III+IV+V+VI = \text{Thesis}$$

A heading with its subheadings is the equivalent of a paragraph with its supporting details.

$$IV = A+B+C$$
$$C = 1+2$$

- The outline demonstrates relatively equal sub-headings.

- Note how, in each category, the subheadings, taken together, equal their main headings.

- The outline moves from the general to the specific.

- It is arranged by order of importance, from the basics of nonverbal communication to the more specific aspects and how they can be read, building toward reader understanding.

Remember that the outline maps out the body of the paper. It will be your paragraph-by-paragraph guide for writing the draft.

Step 9: Write the Draft

Use the following guidelines as you write the first draft of your paper.

General Suggestions

If you write with pen and paper, write on every other line and only on one side of your paper. That way, you'll be able to take notes and make corrections easily. If you write at the computer, set the format command for double spacing. Make sure to save everything—even apparently irrelevant notes and early drafts. If you're working on a computer, save two copies of your writing—for example on a disk *and* on your hard drive—just to be on the safe side. Your earlier drafts and notes may also come in handy later as you revise or as you try to locate specific information from sources.

Write the Introduction

Make a conscious effort in your introduction to attract reader interest. Use one of the following techniques for an effective introduction:

- Startle the reader with facts or statistics.
- Ask a provocative question.
- Use a quotation, adage, or proverb.
- Describe a compelling condition or situation.

(If you use any of these first four techniques be sure to make the connection to your topic and thesis clear. You might also want to return to what you stated or asked when you write your conclusion to strengthen your use of the technique.)

- Use a story or conversation to introduce an event.
- Explain a conflict or inconsistency.
- State your thesis in the introduction, usually in the final sentence.

Write the Body Paragraphs

Use the following general guidelines for writing effective body paragraphs:

- Make your paragraphs correspond to your outline or your revised outline.
- Follow the organization established in your outline or your revised outline.
- Include in each paragraph a stated or implied topic sentence.
- Use your notes and research sources to develop support for each paragraph.

- Maintain unity, i.e. make sure all the details and analysis in a paragraph are about the same idea, the idea in the topic sentence.

- Integrate material from your notes smoothly into your own writing, without making it sound like ideas from research are your own, of course.

- Blend quoted material into your own sentences. Change words and use square brackets where necessary.

- Use tables and figures that stand alone, but your text must be clear without the tables or figures. Blend references to tables and figures into your text.

- Use transitional words, phrases, sentences, and paragraphs to connect ideas within and between paragraphs.

- Omit irrelevant material that does not support any of the main ideas from your notes.

Use temporary citations as you write the body paragraphs, and be sure to list the source and page number for all information.

- Use a kind of shorthand from your notes: the source number and the page number from the upper-right corner, the color code, the heading, or the file name.

- For instance, "3-17" is a shorthand temporary citation for page 17 from the source labeled with the number 3. "Blue-35" is shorthand for page 35 of the source that was color coded blue.

Cite anything that comes from either a primary or secondary resource.

- Be sure to enclose the exact words of a source in quotation marks.
- Before you finish with a note card, double check for quotation marks.
- Cite others' ideas and opinions, even if you've put them in your words.
- Cite little-known facts, even if they are easily proven.

Do not cite

- personal opinions and interpretations.
- well-known facts.

If in doubt, cite. Better safe than sorry.

Study a Model Paragraph and Note Cards

The following illustrate how notes become the text of your paper. Notice, also, the temporary citations.

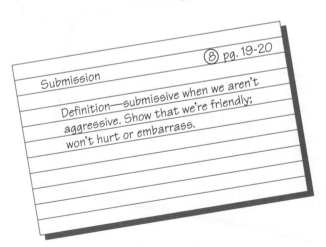

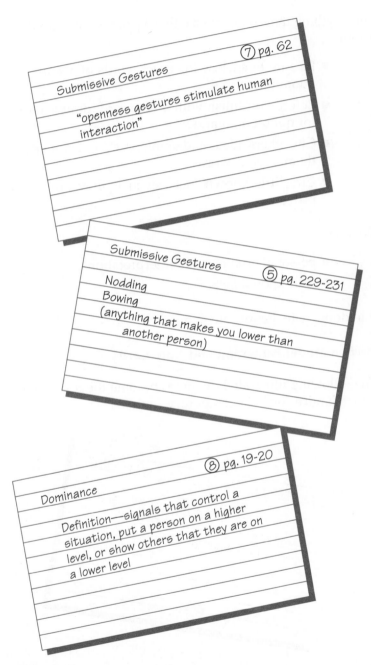

⑦ pg. 62

Submissive Gestures

"openness gestures stimulate human interaction"

Submissive Gestures

⑤ pg. 229-231

Nodding
Bowing
(anything that makes you lower than another person)

⑧ pg. 19-20

Dominance

Definition—signals that control a situation, put a person on a higher level, or show others that they are on a lower level

Paragraph

> On a basic level, human nonverbal communication con-
> sists of submission signals and dominance signals.
> Submission, when discussing nonverbal communication,
> means that people show they are not a threat and are
> not trying to hurt or embarrass other people (8, 19-20).
> The best studied facial behaviors in humans are
> smiles, which are an example of a submissive signal.
> This is because a smile shows that somebody is
> friendly and open to conversation; smiles and "open-
> ness gestures stimulate human interaction" (7, 62).
> Some other submission signals humans make include
> nodding—similar to bowing, or making oneself lower—
> (5, 229-231), and tilting the head, as when one is
> listening (5, 233-235). While submissive signals show
> that people are open to others and are not aggressive,
> dominance signals send a different message. Dominance
> signals are used to control a situation or to show
> others that they are submissive (8, 19-20). People
> send dominance signals through such actions like
> putting their hands on their hips to appear bigger
> (5, 237) or rocking on the balls of their feet to
> appear taller (4, 21-22).

Conclude Your Paper Effectively

Use one or more of the following techniques to effectively
conclude your paper.

- Provide a summary.
- Reach a conclusion.

- Make an observation.
- Issue a challenge.
- Refer to the introduction.

Once you finish a draft of your paper, set it aside for later revision. Meanwhile, however, you may want to ask a peer editor to read your draft and suggest ways you might improve upon each of the guidelines listed previously.

Step 10: Revise the Draft

After you put distance between you and your paper, you are ready to revise. Use these questions to check for areas needing revision.

Revision Checklist

❑ Do I do in my paper what the thesis statement says I will, i.e., answer the research question?

❑ Do I have a defensible reason for arranging paragraphs in the order I do?

❑ Did I follow my outline or its revision?

❑ Have I maintained the same attitude throughout my paper?

❑ Are all of my paragraphs well written?

■ Does each have a topic sentence, stated or implied?

■ Does each include enough supporting details to defend its topic?

■ Does each paragraph maintain unity, i.e., does every detail included support the topic sentence?

■ Do transitional words, phrases, or sentences connect ideas within paragraphs?

■ Does each paragraph have a concluding idea or sentence (where needed)?

❏ Do transitional words, phrases, or sentences connect ideas between paragraphs?

❏ When I combine the topic sentences from each of the paragraphs, do they logically equal the thesis statement?

❏ Have I written grammatically sound sentences, avoiding fragments, run-ons, comma splices, dangling and misplaced modifiers, and redundancies?

❏ Have I used parallel structures for coordinating elements?

❏ Have I varied my sentences by length?

❏ Have I varied my sentences by structure?

❏ Do my sentences create emphasis for important points?

❏ Did I check for accurate word choice?

❏ Did I check the grammar, mechanics, and usage?

Step 11: Prepare the Final Draft

As you prepare the final draft, follow these guidelines for general form, first page formatting, citations, and the Works Cited page.

General Form

See the model beginning on page 64, which illustrates the following form.

- Use good quality 8 1/2" x 11" white paper, printed on only one side.
- Double-space the entire paper, including long quotations and the Works Cited page.

- Maintain a one-inch margin on all four sides of all pages.
- Maintain a running head made up of your last name and the page number one-half inch from the top of each page, with page numbers flush with the right margin.
- Indent five spaces for each paragraph.
- Avoid having a single line of a paragraph appear at the bottom or top of a page.
- If you have tables or figures, put them as close as possible to the text they support or illustrate.
- If you quote poetry, quote up to three poetic lines by using quotation marks around the quoted work and separating the lines of poetry with the slash (/) mark. If you quote more than three lines, treat the poetry as a long quotation and maintain the poetic form.

Formatting the First Page

Research papers generally do not require a title page. (If yours does, see page 57.) Thus, on the first page of your text at the left margin, enter the following identifying details one inch from the top, on four double-spaced lines:

- your name
- your teacher's name
- course title
- due date

Double-space after the due date and enter the title, centered on the page. Use only initial uppercase letters but use initial lowercase letters for prepositions, articles, and coordinating conjunctions. Do not use quotation marks or underscore or italics.

If your paper requires a title page, include three pieces of information, balanced left to right and top to bottom: title, author, and course identification (title).

If your paper requires an outline page, use correct format and number the pages with lowercase Roman numerals.

Citations

Include citations after every quotation, précis, or paraphrase.

After any quotation, précis, or paraphrase, enter a space (as between words). Then in parentheses, write the source name and the page number.

Place parenthetical citations in the sentence where a pause would naturally occur: at the end of a sentence, at the end of a clause, at the end of a phrase.

Use the author's last name to indicate the source.

Example:

> Eye contact not only shows whether a person understands a message, but also signals a person's readiness to communicate (Leathers 42-43).

If there are two authors, use both last names.

Example:

> For example, people from rural areas have larger personal and social zones than those raised in cities (Pease and Pease 204-205).

If there is no author, use the title, shortened if possible. Use quotation marks or italics as appropriate for the title.

Example:

> Looking at the ground may signal that somebody is not interested in the conversation ("Eight Things").

If you use more than one work by a given author, identify both the author and the work. Separate the author's name from the title with a comma.

Example:

> The person, if seated, might swing or tap his or her leg (Fast, *Body Language* 45).

Use no punctuation between the name of the source and the page number.

Place sentence-end punctuation immediately after the close parenthesis.

Place close quotation marks before the open parenthesis.

NOTE

If you need to provide a title for a parenthetical citation (no author is listed or you are using more than one source from an author), you can shorten the title to minimize the disruption to your writing.

For example, you could shorten the title *The Definitive Book of Body Language* to *Definitive Book*.

If the author's name appears in the text of the paper, place only the page number in parentheses.

Example:

>Research conducted by Meeren, Heijnsbergen, and de Gelder shows that the "integration of affective information from a facial expression and the accompanying body language is a mandatory automatic process . . ." (16518).

If the quotation ends with an ellipsis, insert the parenthetical citation after the close of the quotation marks but before the final period. See example immediately above.

If you use indirect information, acknowledge the secondary source in the citation. If possible, use the original source for authenticity. Use the abbreviation "qtd." for "quoted."

Example:

>Michael Argyle states, "Too little eye contact is interpreted as not paying attention" (qtd. in Fast 10).

If a summary comes from several sources, all sources appear in a single parenthetical reference. Separate listed sources with semicolons.

Example:

>People use their first encounters with strangers to read nonverbal cues about such things as income, personal preferences, grooming habits, and career status (Wainwright 148; Quilliam 19; Calero 127).

In citing classic literary works, which are available in many editions, instead of citing page numbers, cite chapters, acts and scenes, lines, parts, cantos, etc.

Example:

>In *Hamlet*, the reference "to thine own self be true" (1.3.82) may be one approach to self love.

Works Cited Page

Use the following guidelines to format your Works Cited page.

- Continue the running head on the Works Cited page.

- Center the title "Works Cited" one inch from the top of the page. Do not use quotation marks, underscore, or italics. Use initial upper-case letters.

- Double-space the entire page, both within and between entries.

- Begin the first entry one double space below the title.

- Begin all entries at the left margin, but subsequent lines are indented five spaces.

- Adhere to the format for bibliography notes (see pages 21–31).

- Enter all sources in alphabetical order by the first word on your bibliography card: author's last name or title of article. If a title begins with "A," "An," or "The," alphabetize by the next word.

- Be sure every parenthetical citation included in your text has a corresponding entry on the Works Cited page.

- Maintain a one-inch bottom margin.

- Continue entries on additional pages as necessary, omitting the "Works Cited" title on further pages and beginning the text one inch from the top.

If you cite two or more sources by the same author, follow the rules on the next page.

- Give author's name in only the first entry.
- Subsequent entries indicate the same author by beginning with three hyphens followed by a period.
- Arrange all the publications by the same author in alphabetical order by title.

Example:

> Pease, Allan, and Barbara Pease. *The Definitive Book of Body Language.* New York: Bantam Books, 2006. Print.

> ---. *The Little Book of Men and Women.* London: Orion Books, 2004. Print.

Finally, remember to make a copy of your paper. Save two copies of your paper in two different places.

Step 12: Proofread the Paper

Proofreading is an exacting task. Allow ample time for final checking, and use the following checklist to help you.

Proofreading Checklist

- Look carefully at every word, checking for typing errors or misspellings.
- Avoid dividing words at the ends of lines.
- Check for accurate punctuation.
- Check for grammatical errors, especially errors that you know you have made in the past.
- Check for consistent point of view, most likely third-person point of view.

- Use consistent verb tenses.
- Use correct formatting throughout the text.
- Check the Works Cited page for accuracy:
  - Are the title and running head accurate?
  - Are names spelled correctly?
  - Have you capitalized accurately?
  - Are punctuation marks correct, especially in relationship to other punctuation?
  - Does each entry end with a period?
  - Have you italicized and used quotation marks accurately?
  - Is the list of entries correctly alphabetized?
  - Have you correctly cited multiple works by the same author?
- Check direct quotations to make sure they are accurate.
- Check your text against your notes to make sure you used necessary quotation marks, thus avoiding plagiarism.
- Check for accurate citations, including correctly spelled names and correct page numbers.
- Check that every source cited in your paper is also listed on the Works Cited page.
- Check that only sources cited in your paper are included on the Works Cited page.
- Make sure your paper reflects your best effort.

Analyze a
Complete Model

Blaser 1

Sarah Blaser
Ms. Ewing
English A
18 November 2009

What People Are Really Saying:
The Unspoken Aspects of Communication

Persuasion is a skill everybody will have to use
at some point in life. Maybe a student will try to
convince an English teacher to give him a higher
grade, or perhaps a girl will want her best friend to
believe her side of the story about what happened at a
party. People who need to persuade others spend a lot
of time planning what they're going to say and trying
to choose the right words. But how often do they stop
to think about the body language they will use while
talking? Will they make eye contact? Will they stand
with confidence? Will they smile or stay straight-
lipped? People often forget to consider what messages
they are sending through nonverbal communication—
eye contact, posture, gestures, and facial expressions.
Everybody use these forms of communication
automatically, without realizing it. In fact, while people
speak for about 11 minutes a day, they use an average
of 250,000 facial expressions in the same amount of
time (Pease and Pease 9). Although people may forget
to think about the nonverbal signals they give out, the
people being spoken to *do* notice these signals. An
English teacher will notice if a student is smiling while
pleading for an A, and a best friend will notice if
someone is avoiding eye contact. Because people
automatically make use of nonverbal messages in all
face-to-face encounters, learning to send and interpret

Running head 1/2" from top

Student, teacher, and class identification, 1" from top

Due date, day/month/year

Title, centered; colon separates title from subtitle

Introduction begins with a hook, shows relevance to the reader

Introduction concludes with thesis statement

these messages accurately will improve overall
communication at home, in school, with new
acquaintances, and beyond.

While people are hardwired to "read" nonverbal
communication, that does not necessarily mean that
they do so correctly. People may have the inborn
ability to interpret and produce nonverbal
communication, but they have to learn how to do
it well. This is like spoken communication—people
have vocal chords to speak, but they must learn to
create the different sounds. When babies and children
are learning spoken language, they are also learning
about nonverbal communication. This is proven by
the facts that infants maintain eye contact with their
mothers, favor their mother's language over others',
and recognize and mimic smiles (Segerstråle and
Molnár 10-11). Dale Leathers writes that nonverbal
communication, more than spoken words, is the major
determinant of meaning in interpersonal exchanges
(7). In other words, people take more from each
other's eye contact, gestures, and posture than they do
from what others actually say. When the spoken and
physical messages do not match, the human mind
will favor the nonverbal communication (Calero 89).
Clearly, if people are not aware of their body language,
they may send unintentional messages or misinterpret
messages sent by others.

On a basic level, human nonverbal communication
consists of submission signals and dominance signals.
Submission, when discussing nonverbal communication,
means that people show they are not a threat and are
not trying to hurt or embarrass other people (Quilliam

Transition into first body paragraph

Co-authors

Author's name included in text; page only in parentheses

Topic sentence

Blaser 3

19-20). The best studied facial behaviors in humans are smiles, which are an example of a submissive signal. This is because a smile shows that somebody is friendly and open to conversation; smiles and "openness gestures stimulate human interaction" (Leathers 62). Some other submission signals humans make include nodding—similar to bowing, or making oneself lower—(Pease and Pease 229-231), and tilting the head, as when one is listening (Pease and Pease 233-235). While submissive signals show that people are open to others and are not aggressive, dominance signals send a different message. Dominance signals are used to control a situation or to show others that they are submissive (Quilliam 19-20). People send dominance signals through such actions like putting their hands on their hips to appear bigger (Pease and Pease 237) or rocking on the balls of their feet to appear taller (Calero 21-22).

Understanding when to use dominance and submission signals could mean the difference between success and failure. For example, when entering a superior's office—like the school principal's office—using dominance signals would offend the superior, and that might mean that a request would not be granted, or a reprimand would be made more severe. However, at other times dominant signals may be better. A girl walking down a dark street alone will be an easier target for an attacker if she displays submissive signals rather than dominant ones. In this situation, a girl who holds an upright posture, maintains a confident gaze, and keeps her arm powerfully over her bag will discourage a potential attacker (Quilliam 50).

Quotation run in with text

Transition within paragraph

Two sources used in one sentence

One-word transition

Blaser 4

In addition to sending out dominance and submission signals, claiming territory is an important aspect of nonverbal communication. People commonly refer to their "personal space," a sort of imaginary bubble around their bodies; this is their territory. In the animal kingdom, territories are easy to see. One example is birds sitting on power lines. The birds sit a certain distance from each other, and often the distance between each bird is equal, within a few inches (Calero 16). As with dominance and submission signals, humans can regulate interaction by either allowing others into a personal space or by keeping them out (Leathers 78).

> Common knowledge, does not need to be cited

> Repeating idea in topic sentence; shows unity

The size of a person's territory is based on what kind of interaction is taking place, and so different rules apply for whether someone has intruded on another's space. There are four zones of space: the intimate zone, the personal zone, the social zone, and the public zone. An explanation of each zone is as follows:

1. Intimate zone: 6 to 18 inches from the body, can be entered only by those with whom people are very close such as loved ones, friends, parents, etc.

2. Personal zone: 18 to 48 inches away from the body, the distance at which people stand at parties and other social functions.

3. Social zone: 4 to 12 feet from the body, reserved for strangers like a salesperson or the plumber.

4. Public zone: over 12 feet from the body, used when addressing a large group. (Pease and Pease 194-195)

> Long quotation is introduced with a colon

> No quotation marks are used with long quotations, and the parentheses come after the period

Blaser 5

Coming too close, say standing or sitting too close to people at a party, will create a reaction in them. If seated, they might swing or tap a leg (Fast 45), or if they are standing they may move backwards (Pease and Pease 239). If people feel their personal space has been invaded and react in these negative ways, they are sending the message that further interaction is not wanted. If the receiver misunderstands the signal, at best, time will be wasted, and at worst, offense will be taken.

A person's upbringing or background can affect the size of each zone. For example, people from rural areas have larger personal and social zones than those raised in cities (Pease and Pease 204-205). This knowledge can be important both in social encounters and in professional encounters. If a city dweller makes a new acquaintance, somebody from a rural area, then the city dweller might assume that the acquaintance doesn't like him or her based on their initial interaction. The acquaintance, however, might simply be acting hostile or aggressive because the acquaintance feels personal space has been invaded. A more significant example might be a college interview. A student from a rural setting may maintain more personal space from the interviewer. The interviewer may then feel a lack of connection and perceive the student as cold or arrogant, which could hurt the student's chances of acceptance.

People have specific rules for space, and they also use eye contact in particular ways to communicate nonverbally. As with reading facial expressions, eye contact is a skill people start practicing in infancy.

Starting the line after the quotation flush with the left margin signals that it is still the same paragraph

Topic sentence serves as a transition and states the main idea of the paragraph

Summarizes two pages from a source

Writer uses specific example to make importance clearer

According to Gordon R. Wainwright, eye contact is
"connected with basic survival patterns, in that
youngsters who could secure and retain eye contact,
and therefore attention, stood the best chance of being
fed and of having their other needs satisfied" (7). The
importance of eye contact continues into adulthood,
when the eyes play a central role during almost every
interaction. Eye contact not only shows whether a
person understands a message, but also signals a
person's readiness to communicate (Leathers 42-43).
If a person is able to see from someone's eyes that a
message is not understood (say someone uses a big
word and gets a blank stare in response), then the
person can adapt the message (like explaining the
same idea with simpler words). Similarly, if a person
can see that someone is avoiding eye contact, then the
person can more successfully interact with others by
approaching only people who are open to interaction.
In addition, eye contact can betray whether somebody
is listening poorly: pretend listening, selectively
listening, or listening self-centeredly (Smith). In other
words, eye contact can show whether people are
listening just because they have to or if people are
listening and absorbing what is being said. Unless eye
contact shows that another person is truly listening, it
may be a good idea to choose a different time for
communicating. Conversely, if someone shows signs of
poor listening, other people may respond negatively or
cut short a conversation.

In studying eye behavior, researchers have
observed certain patterns in most people, especially
during social interaction. During conversation, eye

Parenthetical explanation

One-word transition signaling a second example

Source with no page numbers

Clarifies information from source

Blaser 7

contact is sustained sixty to seventy percent of the time. Holding eye contact for longer—like staring too intently at someone telling a story—can make somebody appear over-interested or aggressive, which will alienate others (Pease and Pease 175-178). The storyteller might begin to wonder if there is something in his or her teeth. In contrast, looking at the ground may signal that somebody is not interested in the conversation ("Eight Things"). Moreover, when socializing, people use the "social gaze," meaning they look at others' faces between the eyes and mouth. People look at other areas of the face in other settings, such as the "power gaze" in business, a gaze aimed between the eyes (Pease and Pease 181). Using the gaze appropriate to a situation or reading another's gaze to determine someone's motives can be helpful. For example, a person probably shouldn't use a power gaze when spending time with friends, but the same person might use it during a class presentation or speech. If the gaze used by others is a "power gaze," then behavior should be formal, but if the "social gaze" is used, then behaving formally might confuse or isolate others.

Unsigned article

People also follow a predictable pattern of eye behavior when social interactions first begin. If somebody comes into a room, it is natural for the other people in the room to look at that person briefly (Pease and Pease 9). This is helpful to know; if a person enters a room filled with staring eyes, it's not because of anything that person has done, but simply because people want to know who has entered their space. Author Susan Quilliam recommends that when

Topic sentence signals a change; the writer will now discuss initial meetings in social interaction

Blaser 8

entering a room, people should do so purposefully, with open posture, and they should make eye contact with others. This shows others that the person entering the room is ready for interaction. People who return the eye contact are approachable, and those are the people to connect with in conversation (35). If people recognize the person entering a room, they will show an "eyebrow flash," during which the eyebrows widen slightly. Again, Quilliam recommends that the eyebrow flash be used to signal openness. She further advises that if one receives this look of recognition, one should not turn away (19). Doing so may offend the person who sent the flash, and that person may feel snubbed or ignored.

Another aspect of nonverbal behavior people can use is leg and foot placement. Legs and feet can reveal much about people since these are less susceptible to control than other parts of the body. Allan and Barbara Pease observe:

> The farther away from the brain a body part is positioned, the less awareness [people] have of what it is doing. For example, most people are aware of their faces and what expressions and gestures they are displaying and [people] can even practice some expressions. . . . After [the] face, [people] are less aware of [the] arms and hands, then [the] chest and stomach, and [people] are least aware of [the] legs and almost oblivious to [the] feet. (209)

Because the movement and placement of feet and legs are almost unconscious, they can send messages that

Word changed to fit grammatically is enclosed in square brackets

Long quotations are set off with an extra indent but are still double-spaced

Ellipses shows omission

Blaser 9

people may not volunteer, and they can tell much about people's true thoughts or feelings.

Researchers identify four basic leg and foot positions, each showing a general attitude. The first is when a person stands or sits with legs parallel, which implies neutrality. The second is a dominant position, when the legs are apart, either while standing or while sitting (212). Susan Quilliam explains this by noting that people will place their legs this way only when they are comfortable or feeling superior, since the position exposes vulnerable areas of the body. Quilliam extends her analysis to the feet, stating that feet turned outward are a sign of confidence and feet turned inward may be a sign of insecurity (214-215).

The third leg and foot arrangement has more to do with orientation than with actual position. According to Barbara and Allan Pease, "the foot points where the mind most wants to go" (214). This means that a jiggling foot might indicate that a person wants to leave or that feet will point toward the most desirable person in a group (Pease and Pease 284-285). Lastly, the fourth position is with legs or feet crossed or curled around each other, which betrays closed-mindedness or a need to protect oneself (Fast 138). If people are exhibiting these, it might not be the best time to try and convince them of something, or a gentle approach might be best to ease anxiety.

Although people are often unaware of their leg and feet movements, it is possible to recognize them and bring them under conscious control. What's more,

> Signal words help readers keep track of the four items in the list

> Cited material concludes the paragraph

> Signal word shows the final item in the list

Blaser 10

a person can interpret and even change the mostly
unconscious feet and leg movements of others for more
effective communication. When people interact with
each other, they see expressed emotions and often
mirror those emotions, which then elicit the same
feelings in others (Segerstråle and Molnár 14). In
fact, when people see an emotion expressed, mirror
neurons (brain cells) activate to produce the same
emotion in themselves (Kelly et al. 328). Essentially, if
a person wants to create a certain response or feeling
in another, then that person simply needs to show
that feeling. For example, if somebody moved to a
new town and wanted to meet new people, say at an
after-school club, it would not help to sit with legs
crossed since that position does not communicate
openness, and the club members might not feel open
to this new person in response. Similarly, if a person
saw that an opponent was sitting with legs crossed
during an important negotiation, then the person may
need to communicate more openness in body language
to get the opponent to "open up" to the negotiation.

Hand and arm movements are similar to leg and
feet movements and frequently communicate the same
messages. Just as crossed legs make people feel
protected, so are crossed arms a sign that a person
feels threatened or that a person does not want to
interact (Pease and Pease 90). Conversely, open arms
or exposed palms (originally meant to show that a
person was not carrying any concealed weapons)
communicate honesty and approachability (Pease and
Pease 31). Reading crossed arms or clenched hands
correctly can lead to greater success in a number of

Helps to explain/define technical term

Phrase shows that an illustration of the point will follow

New area of discussion is connected strongly to the one that came just before

Blaser 11

settings, especially when making a request or trying to build rapport. If a student approaches a teacher to discuss a grade, for example, and the teacher has her arms crossed, it would help the student to get the teacher to uncross her arms. The student can ask the teacher to examine a paper as the teacher will have to uncross her arms to hold the paper. In a social setting, initiating open movements with the hands and arms will encourage openness on the other person's part as that person becomes more comfortable and starts to mirror the open gestures. During a conflict, also, if one person starts to use open gestures and a non-threatening tone of voice, the other person will respond in the same way and the conflict will more likely be resolved (National Crime Prevention Council).

According to body-language expert Dale Leathers, gestures—whether open or closed—are another valuable source of nonverbal communication; because they are more numerous than other channels, like posture, they can reveal more information (60). Some common hand-to-face gestures include the following: a hand supporting the head, which signals boredom; a hand lightly supporting the head with one finger pointing upward along the side of the face, which signals evaluation; a thumb supporting the head with a finger pointing up, which indicates negative thoughts; and stroking the chin, which means that a decision is about to be made (Pease and Pease 155-159). These gestures can be especially helpful in a situation like an interview for an after-school or summer job. A job candidate can read the interviewer's nonverbal messages and adjust accordingly (Quilliam 108). The

Application of ideas to support thesis: using body language can make communication more effective

Organization as the author of a source

Occupation given to lend authority to source

Colon used to introduce a list

Semicolons used to separate long items in a list

Blaser 12

candidate might want to stop talking if the interviewer is supporting the head with a hand. The same is true if the interviewer is showing signs of negative thoughts. If an interviewer strokes the chin or shows signs of evaluation, the candidate can step in with additional positive information to try to sway the decision in a favorable direction. This would be far more effective than waiting for the decision and then trying to change it, which might make the candidate seem aggressive or desperate.

Nonverbal cues can be used in a variety of situations and, if they are used and understood correctly, they can improve a person's overall communication skills. Dominant or submissive postures and gestures are appropriate in different situations, and knowing whether one is sending a message of power or compromise is important to avoid offending others or to build relationships with others. Eye behaviors, hand and feet positions, and arm and hand movements all communicate thoughts and feelings, whether people are aware of them or not. On a subconscious level, these thoughts and feelings are interpreted by others, and so people will more clearly convey meaning if they learn to control the nonverbal messages they send. When reading messages sent by others, it is important to place all nonverbal communication in context so that it is not misinterpreted. People should account for such factors as cold (if a man has his arms crossed) or modesty (if a woman wearing a skirt crosses her legs) to avoid misreading cues. When reading somebody's body language, a person should look for more than just one

> Conclusion restates ideas from introduction to tie up essay neatly

> New idea introduced to clarify concepts in paper

Blaser 13

signal. So, if a woman has her legs crossed, but the
rest of her body language is open, she is probably
open to interaction. If her gestures are few, however,
she is not making eye contact, and she is not smiling,
then her legs are likely showing a closed attitude.
Whether a person reads nonverbal cues in clusters
or in individual movements, being aware of the common feelings associated with bodily communication
can provide people with additional information
and so create deeper and richer relationships
with others.

Essay ends with a strong concluding statement and leaves the reader with something to consider

Blaser 14

Works Cited

Calero, Henry H. *The Power of Nonverbal Communication*. Los Angeles: Silver Lake Publishing, 2005. Print.

De Gelder, Beatrice. "Towards the Neurobiology of Emotional Body Language." *Nature Reviews Neuroscience* March 2006: 242-249. Print.

"Eight Things to do to Practice Better Communication." *Palo Alto Medical Foundation*. Sutter Health, n.d. Web. 28 Aug. 2009.

Fast, Julius. *Body Language*. New York: M. Evans and Co., 2002. Print.

Kelly, Spencer D., et al. "Putting Language Back in the Body: Speech and Gesture in Three Time Frames." *Developmental Neuropsychology* August 2002: 323-349. Print.

Leathers, Dale G. *Successful Nonverbal Communication*. New York: Macmillan Publishing Company, 1986. Print.

Meeren, Hanneke K. M., Corné C. R. J. van Heijnsbergen, and Beatrice de Gelder. "Rapid Perceptual Integration of Facial Expression and Emotional Body Language." *PNAS* 8 Nov. 2008: 16518-16523. Print.

National Crime Prevention Council. *Making Peace: Tips on Conflict Management*. Washington: National Crime Prevention Council, 2009. PDF File.

Pease, Allan, and Barbara Pease. *The Definitive Book of Body Language*. New York: Bantam Books, 2004. Print.

Quilliam, Susan. *Body Language*. Buffalo: Firefly Books, 2004. Print.

Title of Works Cited page is centered, 1" from top; double space to first entry

Entries arranged alphabetically

Unsigned article alphabetized by title

More than three authors for this article, indicated by "et al."

Colon separates title from subtitle

Digital source

Segerstråle, Ullica, and Peter Molnár, eds. *Nonverbal Communication: Where Nature Meets Culture.* Mahway: Lawrence Erlbaum Associates, Inc., 1997. Print.

Smith, Anita M. "The Communication Gap." *The Institute for Youth Development.* The Institute for Youth Development, n.d. Web. 28 Aug. 2009.

Editors' names used for alphabetization

Indicates no date was provided on this Internet source

Compare Styles: MLA and APA

Some disciplines follow the *Publication Manual of the American Psychological Association* (APA) style for citations. The following guidelines explain the differences between MLA and APA styles.

Parenthetical Citations

APA parenthetical citations follow this style:

- All parenthetical citations include the author's name and the date of publication.
- Page numbers are included only if reference is made in the paper to a specific page or chapter or if a quotation is included.
- When page numbers are included, they are preceded by the designation *p.* or *pp.*
- Items in the citation are separated by commas.

Examples:

(Norvell, 1992)
(Norvell, 1992, p. 16)
(Norvell, 1992, pp. 16-17)

Reference Pages

Instead of referring to a Works Cited page, the APA style uses the term Reference Page. Still, the format is quite similar to MLA, with the following exceptions:

- The date of publication follows, parenthetically, the author's name.
- Quotation marks are omitted from periodical article titles.

- Only first word and proper nouns of titles are capitalized; the first word of a subtitle is capitalized.
- Volume numbers of periodicals are italicized.
- Entries are double-spaced with hanging indentation, the second and subsequent lines being indented only three, rather than five, spaces.

Examples:

Carlson, Ruth Kearney. (1995, March). Poetry as a reading aid: An introduction. *Elementary English, 62,* 273-274.

Norwell, George W. (1990). *The reading interests of young people.* Boston, MA: D.C. Health and Company.

Use whichever style your teacher requests, and maintain consistency throughout your paper.

Index